# How to Market Yourself

Being Empowered to Succeed

## Laura Lynn Kerner

# Introduction

Using marketing principles to teach students how to market themselves came when I found that students didn't see any reason why they should take a marketing course. Since it was a required course for all students in Business and some in Arts & Science, I started looking for ways to engage these students.

I thought if I could make the course applicable to them personally, it might work. I implemented the idea and asked for student critiques at the end of the semester. It was rough at first but tweaking the course per their suggestions made it better. Then I wrote this book to explain the concept. Students really liked it, easily got the concept and began sharing the book with friends and family.

I learned a valuable teaching lesson by doing this. The more you make a course personally relevant, students remember the concepts better and they grow both personally and professionally. I found that applying proven business management practices to our lives helps us make better decisions and thus manage our lives successfully.

This book teaches you how to apply marketing principles to market yourself. The book also contains principles I discovered in my own personal journey of overcoming low self-esteem. All the principles have been tried and tested either in multiple classes over many semesters or via personal experience.

This is a revision of the original book and I've added more content and updated it. I've included things I've learned from students applying the principles and from others who have written books, which are listed in the suggested readings at the end of the book. It is also based on things I have learned from my own personal struggle with lack of self-esteem to a position of self-assurance and confidence.

This book was written for 3 reasons: for students and others who want to be successful, for my children and grandchildren, and for others who want to learn how to be empowered to be successful. It is my desire that by reading this book you will become empowered to succeed.

*Dedicated to the friends who have stood by me, supported me and continued steadfastly in their friendship with me through all the difficult and joyful times in my life.*

*Linda Pannell*
*Betty Whitten*
*Susan Morris*
*Shera Owen*
*Jimmie Marshall*
*Marion Madison*

# Acknowledgements

This book is a culmination of work from both professional and personal experience. Professionally I created a new method for teaching marketing principles. Personally I worked through low self-esteem issues and incorporated good business practices in my personal life. Along the way there were many people who made contributions to my life both professionally and personally. Without their contributions this book would have never been written.

Thanks to Jimmie Marshall for all the times she listened to me when I had a 'pity party' or felt like I was a 'victim.' She role-played with me as I struggled to become assertive and stand up for myself. Jimmie has also reviewed every document I have ever written and created illustrations when I needed them. She has always supported me and my family and goes above and beyond in that support. It would be my wish that everyone in the world could have a friend like Jimmie.

Thanks to Tracy Hicks who has consistently supported me in all my publication endeavors with her professional work and creative designs. She has always met my deadlines even when short and done so with excellence and dedication.

Thanks to three former students, Shelana Dorn, Gabrielle Clark and Angela Langston, who encouraged me to teach others how to market themselves.

Thanks to my cousin, Dr. James McLemore, who has graciously edited this book.

Thanks to all the students who took my Principles of Marketing classes and critiqued them so that I could constantly improve my teaching methods. The majority of students embraced the new concepts of using marketing principles to market themselves. They also told me what they liked and didn't like and how to make my classes better.

Thanks to Gerald Kimbrough who vented with me about the difficult job situation we were in as we drove to and from work. I learned from Gerald's persistence and perseverance that you can achieve your vision in life.

Thanks to Richard Blankenship who taught me that how I saw myself was not who I really was. He also taught me to define myself by identifying those things that I liked about myself. He helped me change my life, my world and my self-esteem.

To all the unnamed people who made my life difficult but in the end it was those hardships that forced me look at myself, change who I was and set boundaries for my life. Without them I would have never learned what I've learned and been able to write this book. Difficulties can make you stronger if you learn from them and become a victor. Give up being a victim and to let go of your "pity parties."

# Contents

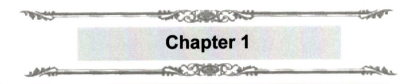

# Chapter 1

# What is Marketing?

The standard definition of marketing: it is the process of planning and executing a concept (product), pricing, promoting, and distributing that product which can be an idea, product, service, place or person (YOU). Marketing is used to create places where money is transferred between the buyer and seller that will satisfy individuals and organizational goals.

Let's apply that definition personally. In order to market yourself you have to develop a planning process whereby you create your product, price your product, promote it and distribute it. YOU are the product.

Product: To develop your product, you will need to start by determining what your vision is for your life. Then make a plan to achieve that vision and implement the plan. In light of the vision you have for your life and the career or job you want, you will need to develop your product, which is YOU. You will need to develop your product into someone who meets the qualifications for the job.

Price: You have a professional price (or value) that is determined by how you measure up to the qualifications for the job you want. Your personal price (value) is determined by how you respond to the way others treat you.

Place: Put yourself in the right places at the right time to be noticed.

Promotions: Promote yourself by telling people who you are and how you can be a "benefit" to them.

Whether you're marketing a product, a service, an idea, a place or person – YOU, you must decide what You as a product want to be, put a value on that product, be in the right place at the right time and promote yourself in ways to accomplish your goals and ultimately your vision.

This book will describe in detail how you use the marketing principles of product, price, place and promotion to achieve the vision you created for your life. Marketing strategy is important to use to be successful.

*You can use marketing principles to market yourself.*

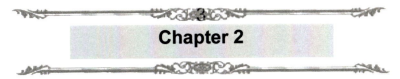

# Chapter 2

## What is the Purpose of Marketing?

Marketing is designed to accomplish specific goals: to get more customers, to make more profits, to get more share of the market. For you it might be to get a job, to get promoted, to obtain more money, to get your ideas across to your boss. Whatever your goals are understanding marketing can help you accomplish these.

Good marketers start with their objectives and they always listen to customer feedback to improve their product, its distribution or service. You will need to do the same thing. Ask for honest feedback on your product from friends, colleagues, and family, people you trust.

The bottom line is that companies use marketing to be successful. Success in business means that the company will continue to operate and grow.

Successful companies can offer jobs, give raises to employees and provide good working conditions. They can share increased profits with investors and provide raises for their employees. The company may have funds to contribute to the community, help with the ecology, or other social needs in the world.

Success for YOU as an individual means first and foremost that you are happy with your product, YOURSELF. You have healthy relationships with others – family, friends, and peers and that you are achieving your goals – personal, financial, and social.

Through your marketing plan and execution of that plan you can be successful in creating YOU as a distinctive brand with value and worth. You can put yourself in the right places at the right times, promote yourself and achieve the results you desire.

*Companies use marketing principles to be more successful. You can do the same thing.*

3

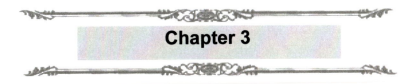

# Chapter 3

## The 4 Ps of Marketing

In Chapter 1 you might have noticed the reference to Product, Price, Place and Promotion. These are referred to as the 4 Ps of marketing.

**Products** - can be a material item (something tangible – milk, shoes, guns) or a service (something used – airline tickets, cleaning, medical care) or a combination of both. Products can also be an idea, a place or person and the person can be YOU.

**Price** - is the value that is put on the product. The quality, image and/or benefits that a product offers influences how much a consumer is willing to pay (or exchange) to have the product.

**Place** – is the channel or route used to get the product to the destination. Being in the right place at the right time gives the product a greater chance of sales (being bought). It involves the medium used to deliver the message about the product. Place (when the product is you) can be places like the internet, TV, radio, magazines, etc.

**Promotion** – is the communication efforts (all the activities) used to raise awareness of the product or brand leading to the generation of sales and the creation of brand loyalty. It is the "message" about what benefits the product has. Advertising, sales promotions, public relations are promotional efforts.

> *Marketing is about the 4 Ps:*
> *Product, Price, Place and Promotion.*

# Chapter 4

## The First Step in Marketing Yourself

The first step that a company takes when starting a business is to decide what they want to accomplish. They have a vision for what they want to be and where they want their company to go.

This should also is the first step you take. You need to ask the question: "What do I want out of life?" Your vision should be what you dream of, what you hope for. It is how you see your future. It is a visual description of the aspirations you have of what you want to achieve and accomplish now and in the future. A vision is your dreams in picture form.

If you don't have a vision it is like getting in a car and driving without a destination. If you don't have a destination, you'll just drive around aimlessly. We do that in life when we don't have a vision.

Visions are the pictures you have in your mind about your future. What kind of job you want. The spouse you want. The car you want. What you want for your children. How much money you want to make and save.

Once you have the visual picture then you should make it specific. You need to be able to express your vision in measurable terms; like – finishing college in _____, marrying a man/woman with these qualities_____, obtain a job in _____ paying $_____, buy a house costing $_____, saving $ _____million for retirement. Your vision needs to be SPECIFIC.

*Start dreaming!!*
*Dreams are 'all that you can imagine'.*

Don't dream small.  Most people can only imagine what they've known or  previously seen.  Some people are afraid to dream because they don't feel like they deserve to have more.  Don't feel this way because you have worth and value and you were created to be successful.  Don't limit yourself to small dreams that are restricted by what you've known or seen.

*Create Your Vision*
*Do it Today!*

Find pictures that represent what you want, the house, the car, the spouse, the job, the amount of money.  Put these on a poster board or in a power point presentation.  If you create your vision on paper put it where you can see it every day and be sure to look at it every day.  Looking at it every day should continuously inspire you to work toward that vision.

**Creating your vision in pictorial form imprints an image on your brain that is easier to remember.  Get your destination set and go for it.**

# Chapter 5

## The Second Step in Marketing Yourself

The second step in marketing yourself may be more difficult than the first. It is deciding what your purpose or what your mission is in life. Purpose is the meaning of your life. It is your mission. Your overall purpose or mission may remain the same. However, during different periods in your life your specific purpose (mission) may change. For example, when you are going to school you mission may be different than it will be when you are married and raising children.

Deciding what your purpose (mission) is may start with you writing down what your values are. Values are your principles, your standards of behavior; those things that are most important to you. The character qualities that you value and attribute worth to.

**Values serve as the moral compass for our lives.**

Values set the boundaries for our lives. They serve as the guard-rails along the road we travel. They keep us safely on the road so that we reach our destination (our vision) and keep us on course. Robert Steven Kaplan in his book, "What You're Really Meant to Do" states, "If you want to reach your potential, you must be willing to figure out what you believe and have the courage to act on your beliefs. You need to make a leap of faith that, even though justice may not prevail at a given point in time, ultimately it will prevail."

Write down your values and review them periodically. Your values help you make the right choices and right choices get you to your destination without wasting time recovering from bad choices. They will help you reach your ultimate potential. Example of some values:

1. To live above reproach.
   (having conduct that would not cause disappointment, displeasure, or would discredit me, my friends or my family)

2. To always be honest.
   (free from fraud or deception; being genuine and real)

3. To always tell the truth.
   (sincerity in action, character and utterance- being trusted)

4. To have integrity. (having strong moral principles; always doing the "right thing" and "doing it right," not giving in to peer or authority pressure for self- preservation.)

5. To treat others with respect and dignity regardless of position, appearance, social standing or monetary worth, knowing that no one is any better than you are, nor are you any better than anyone else.

The list can go on and on. I know someone whose list consists of 28 values.

By starting with our values we set our moral compass and our boundaries. Our values set the framework for our mission (purpose).

I've come up with what I think could be everyone's purposes in life:

1.   To make yourself better
2.   To help someone else make their life better.
3.   To make the world a better place, even if it is by planting a tree, giving someone a smile or saving a whale.

When you live above reproach, when you tell the truth, when you have integrity and treat everyone with respect, regardless of position, appearance, or monetary worth, then you can say that you are a person of value. My daddy use to describe such a person by saying, "He is a good man or he has a good name."

When you are that kind of person and strive to become even better and to help others to be better and contribute to making the world a better place, you could say you are fulfilling your purpose (mission) in life.

It is very important to have a purpose and to live with purpose. None of us know how long we have on earth but if we can live our "dash" with purpose and passion, we will leave knowing we have fulfilled our reason for being (our purpose) on this earth.

I recommend your reading the poem "The Dash" by Linda Ellis and/or watch the video about "The Dash" on the Simple Truths website.

# Chapter 6

## The 1st P in Marketing - Know and Like Your Product

Products and services are constantly being evaluated and judged by consumers asking such questions as: how does the product look, what will it do for me, what benefit will I get from it or how will I look if I have it – will I have more status, will I be more attractive or will somebody think I'm important?

If you judge and evaluate the products or services you purchase, how then do you judge and evaluate yourself? You are constantly marketing yourself, whether you know it or not, and the image you have of yourself influences how you present your product to the world. Some people have difficulty speaking to others; some hold their head down and don't make eye contact. Others cross one arm and hold onto the other arm. What is this body language conveying about the image they have of themselves?

What is your image of yourself?

You probably first think about how you look. The media constantly bombards us with messages about appearance. Entertainers, celebrities, news anchors, TV personalities all look perfect. Ads portray beautiful women as being thin with perfect hair, eyes, and skin; men are handsome and muscular.

If you get your image by comparing yourself to the media's image of beautiful and handsome, how do you measure up? Academic studies reveal that the media's emphasis on appearance does affect our level of self-esteem. If the media affects our self image are there other influences that affect our self- image?

Below is a table listing people or things which may influence your feelings about who you are. What these people say to you or how they treat you may greatly affect how you feel about yourself and, thus, what you think about yourself. Your feelings may be negative or positive.

Write down the feelings you have about yourself obtained from the sources listed below:

| Source | Feelings |
|---|---|
| Mother | |
| Father | |
| Sisters | |
| Brothers | |
| Teachers | |
| Friends | |
| TV and Internet | |
| Entertainment/Athletic Idols | |
| Magazines ads | |
| Celebrities & Fashion Models | |
| Music | |
| Step-Father | |
| Step- Mother | |
| Coaches | |
| Aunts | |
| Uncles | |
| Family Friends | |
| Other | |

After you complete this exercise, write down how these feelings shaped how you think about yourself now. What is your self image based on these messages?

_____

_____

_____

_____

_____

_____

Your self-image, which was shaped by what others said or did to you, created thoughts in your mind about who you are and those thoughts play over and over in your mind like a continuous stream of music or a non-stop playing CD.

The question is should your self-image come solely from the previously listed sources? If not, then where should your self-image or self-worth come from?

> *You can never sell your product (YOU) successfully if you don't think you are a good product.*

Successful sales people:
- believe in their product and/or service
- like their product and/or service
- think that their product or service has value and worth

Do you
- like yourself?
- believe in yourself?
- feel that you have worth and value?

If not, then what?

1. Recognize that the negative feelings and thoughts you have about yourself that came from others is not necessarily true. Professionals call this "issues of family origin" meaning you may have self- esteem, self-concept or perception issues because of what was said to you, how you were treated or the level of dysfunction in the environment you lived in or were exposed to.

2. Recognize that the negative feeling and the negative thinking you have about yourself does not have to continue.

3. Recognize that these negative feelings and thoughts can change.

> *If you don't like yourself, you can change that.*

How can you change what you think about yourself? How do you come to like yourself? How do you believe in yourself and feel you are valuable? How do you overcome shyness, the lack of self-confidence or low self-esteem, the inability to speak up, being self-conscious, worrying about what other people think about you? How do you stop letting people mistreat you?

The list could go on an on but I believe the answer is in discovering who you really are, not who someone else says you are. You can do this by ejecting the negative CD that is continuously playing in your mind and replace it with a positive one.

How do you do that?

> *Create a picture of who you really are by listing the things you like about yourself.*

Begin by creating your own picture of who you are and I mean "literally" create your own picture. Go to a hobby or art supply store and buy a 14 x 18 stretched canvas and an assortment of different colored tissue paper. You might also want to buy different colored pens. I like gold and silver pens.

Do a SWOT analysis on yourself. In a SWOT analysis you list your Strengths, Weaknesses, Opportunities and Threats. Start with Your strengths.

**Strengths**

• Begin by listing your strengths: character trails, skills or other things you like about yourself. Start by identifying 5 things you like about yourself; i.e. hard worker, sincere, compassionate, determined, honest, etc. As you think of each word, tear off a piece of tissue paper and write that word on the tissue paper and glue it to the stretched canvas board.

You are beginning to create a picture of who you really are by making this collage. As you think of more words continue the process. You are creating a picture of YOU - who you really are, not what someone else says you are. You are also creating that positive thought CD.

16

Hang the picture where you can see it daily. Look at it every day before you walk out of your house. Continue this picture project by adding things you like about yourself to the canvas and looking at it every day until you begin to "delete" the negative words replacing them with positive ones. Your mind is like a CD and you can delete negative thoughts and replace them with positive ones.

When someone says something negative to you or about you, you just say to yourself, "No, that's not true because I am _____ (use a positive opposite word.) As you continue to list the things you like about yourself it should soon become evident that many of the things you list do not relate to appearance. What you begin to see is that WHO you are is more about "what you are inside" than "what you look like outside."

> *Realize that you are unique and have special talents and abilities. You are someone special!*

- Be determined to develop self-esteem. Self-esteem means that you have confidence and satisfaction in yourself.

- You were born with unique "natural talents" which equipped you to succeed in the "good plan" that has been designed for our lives.

- Read and re-read the "10 Steps to Self Esteem."

# 10 Steps to Self Esteem

**1. Take inventory.**
Write down all the good things that you can think about yourself. Keep this          list and add to it every time you think of something good about yourself. Also write down your blessings, your accomplishments and your goals and dreams.

**2. Picture yourself as you want to be and act like you are that person.**
If you bring yourself closer to the image of the person you want to be, that will do wonders for your self-esteem.

**3. Say your name more often.**
Volunteer your own name first in every telephone call and whenever you meet someone new. By paying value to your own name in communication, you are developing the habit of paying value to yourself as an individual. Your name has to be repeated 7 times for it to be remembered.

**4. Sit in front.**
When you attend a class or a meeting, always sit in front. You are better able to listen, learn, and interact with the speaker.

**5. Walk with confidence.**
Make a conscious effort to walk more erectly.

**6. Accept a compliment.**
When anyone pays you a compliment, accept it with a simple, "Thank you."

**7. Keep a "What I did" list.**
You probably already keep a "to do" list, but do you keep a "what I did' list?

**8. Feed your mind.**
Get interested in people and places. Get excited about new things! Read, Read, Read. CEOs of companies generally read around 3 books per month or around 35 per year. How much are you reading?

**9. Use affirmative language.**
When you talk about yourself, use positive language.

**10. Look your best.**
You can't like yourself inside if you don't like yourself outside. Make an effort to present yourself in the best way possible at all times. Feeling good about the way you look has a direct effect on your self-image.

# Every Human Being's
# Bill of Rights

1.      The right to be treated with respect.

2.      The right to have and express your own feelings.

3.      The right to say "no" and not feel guilty.

4.      The right to change your mind.

5.      The right to feel and express anger.

6.      The right to be treated as a capable human being and not be degraded or patronized.

7.      The right to have your needs be as important as the needs of others.

8.      The right to make mistakes.

9.      The right to ask for assistance or help.

10.     The right to make your own decisions and take responsibility for the consequences of those decisions.

## Weaknesses

List any weaknesses that you perceive that you have. Weaknesses may be shyness, procrastination, fear of public speaking, financial issues, anger issues, a people pleaser, lack of leadership skills, etc. The list can go on an on. However, I have never seen a single weakness listed by students that could not be overcome unless it was a physical or medical issue.

At the end of this book there is a list of suggested books to read which can help you with your weaknesses. For example, for people who have procrastination and time management issues I recommend using a scheduler, writing down all the things you have to do, then organizing them in the order of importance and the due dates. Write the due dates on your calendar and schedule other work, appointments, meetings, etc.

When I have a particularly difficult behavioral weakness to overcome, like "getting angry," I use a 'steno pad', the one with the spiral rings at the top and the page is divided in half by a line. On the left side of the page, I write "What I Did" and on the right hand side of the page I write "What I Should Have Done." Then I will study the right hand side of the page. The next time I am again faced with a similar situation I try to practice doing what I had listed under "What I Should Have Done."

Role playing is another helpful exercise. When faced with a particularly difficult weakness, like not standing up for myself, I asked a good friend who knew my situation to role play with me. The friend would create a situation where I needed to stand up for myself or I needed to protect my "boundaries." I then would practice what I should say. I continued doing this until I was able to say what I should say without getting emotional and without having to stop and think about what I needed to say. Later, when I was confronted with a difficult situation I could readily respond, quickly and firmly.

Overcoming weaknesses involves:

1. Acknowledging what your weakness is. "You can't change or heal what you do not acknowledge." Dr. Phillip C. McGraw, Relationship Rescue, page 23.

2. Obtaining knowledge (information) that will help you understand the weakness and help you overcome it. You can do this by researching online or finding books that address the issues. You might also seek professional help.

3. Practice what you've learned over and over and over again.

Remember not to get discouraged. You did not get where you are overnight and you will not get where you want to be overnight.

---

*Perseverance and practice WILL pay off.*
*You can overcome any weakness!!!*

# Threats

Threats are things that can keep you from obtaining your vision. Threats may be things that are preventable, things that can be mitigated (their negative impact could be lessened, if you did something now) or things that would require a contingency plan (a plan of action to deal with it, if it did occur).

Threats may be things like: lack of an education, lack of experience, loss of job, divorce, illness, lack of money, having more than you can do – work, family, and school.

My suggestion is to list the threats and put them in a table and list the ways you can mitigate those threats.  Example:

| Threat | Mitigation Efforts |
|---|---|
| Lack of education | |
| | • Find a job in a company that will pay for my education while I work<br>• Get a job where I can go to school and work<br>• Investigate schools with online courses or take CLEP or DSST exams<br>• Apply for student loans |
| Lack of experience or skills | • Get a job that will give me entry level experience in the field I want to go into<br>• Volunteer at a company that is in the field I want to go into<br>• Volunteer for a not-for-profit organization that will give me experience<br>• Find an apprenticeship<br>• Strategic moonlighting<br>• Obtain certifications in the field |
| Loss of job | • Save at least 10%-25% of income first!  Pay yourself first! |
| Divorce | • Get an education |

| Lack of money | • Get a job – Save money |
|---|---|
| More than I can do | • Prioritize |
| Illness | • Eat right<br>• Exercise<br>• Routine medical checks<br>• Long term disability insurance<br>• Save money |

You will always have threats and risks in your lives. However, if you take examples from successful businesses you will make plans just as they do. They face their threats, try to eliminate them if possible and if not, they try to mitigate them. When they see that a threat can't be eliminated or mitigated they make plans to manage the event and insure themselves against catastrophic ones. Why shouldn't you use these same examples of good business practices and apply them to your life?

## Opportunities

*Opportunities are favorable situations or circumstances that help you obtain your vision and put you in a position to succeed.*

Opportunities can be people like friends, family, a mentor who supports you, encourages you or helps you get ahead in life. An opportunity is having the ability to go to college, the ability to overcome weaknesses, having specific experiences, the opportunity to embrace life positively rather than negatively. These are all opportunities.

Many don't recognize that some of the things we think of as ordinary are really extraordinary opportunities. Every positive in your life provides you with some opportunity. Recognize them, be grateful for them and seize them with gusto and use them to the fullest.

Perhaps the greatest opportunity you have now is that you know your product, YOU, and there are things you like about your product. You know what your weaknesses are and you're going to work on them. You know there will be threats in your life but you will look at them squarely and devise a plan to eliminate them or manage them.

You NOW have the opportunity to improve your product. How exciting that can be.

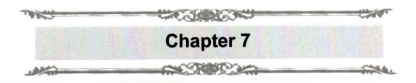

# Chapter 7

## Managing the Product - You

You, hopefully, have recognized now that your self-esteem and your product image should not result from any negative messages you may have received from what others said about you or to you or what they did to you. Neither should your self-concept be influenced by the media's messages about how you should look and what you should have.

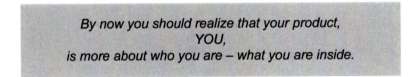

*By now you should realize that your product,*
*YOU,*
*is more about who you are – what you are inside.*

Who you are can be defined by your character traits. Although appearance, personality, educational level, and skills are also a part of you, the more good character traits you add to your product the better you begin to like yourself and believe in yourself. You already possess good character traits and you will find those where you listed your strengths earlier and the things you liked about yourself. As you develop more and more good character traits you become happier and more satisfied with who you are and begin to realize that you do have value and worth. You get better at defining your boundaries - what you will and will not allow people to do to you or say about you.

Below is a list of some good character traits that you may already possess (but don't realize) and some that you would like to add to your product. You can add them to your product by practicing doing them. When a situation occurs that requires you to choose whether you will "do the right thing, because it's right (integrity), make a decision to be a person of integrity and do the right thing. As you continue doing this you will find that you do it automatically without having to think, "I'm going to be a person of integrity. Once you have added this trait, pick another one to add to your product and practice doing it until you've added another good character trait.

There are other things like appearance, education, skills, etc. that help you add additional benefits to your product. They will be discussed later.

## Good Character Traits to Add to Your Product

| Character Trait | Definition | Alternative Definition |
|---|---|---|
| Live above Reproach | Not doing anything that would shame or disgrace your family, friends or yourself. | How you act. What you do or say will never cause you, your family or your friends to be ashamed. |
| Integrity | Always doing the right thing, even when it is not popular, or no one is looking, or it costs you something. | Doing the right thing and doing it right even when you don't feel like it. |
| Diligence | Keep on keeping on! No matter what! | Consistent, energetic, and earnest effort. |
| Honesty | Telling the truth all the time, regardless! | If you tell the truth, you don't have to remember what you said. |
| Excellence | Doing the best you can do! Being the best you can be! | |

| | | |
|---|---|---|
| Consistent | Being the same all the time. Not swayed by pressure. | |
| Reliable | Consistently good in quality or performance | Able to be trusted that you will do what you are supposed to do |
| Compassion | Consistently good in quality or performance | |
| Poise | Graceful or dignified in any situation | Cool under any circum-stances |
| Sincerity | Being real; genuine | Not two-faced |
| Positive | Finding the best in a situation in spite of the circumstances | |
| Confident | Believing in yourself even when you don't feel it. | Acting self assured |
| Courage | Not being afraid to say no | Facing your fear and doing so unafraid! |
| Responsible | Doing what you say you're going to do | |
| Accountable | Taking responsibility for what you do | |
| Kindness | Doing good to or for another | |
| Respectful | Valuing yourself and others | Having spe-cial or high regard for yourself and others |
| Credible | Being believable! | |

| Stable | Remaining quiet and calm no matter what happens! | Not moved by anyone or by your circumstances |
|---|---|---|
| Dependable | Keeping your commitments | Doing what you say you're going to do |
| Self-Control | Not doing or saying everything you want to do or say. Controlling self. | Not giving in to peer pressure but doing what is right |
| Moral | Knowing what's right and wrong and doing what's right | |
| Disciplined work ethic | Showing a consistent, responsible work behavior | |
| Fortitude | Strength to bear pain or adversity with courage | |
| Ethical | Right conduct, personally and professionally | |

A neat project to do while working on adding character traits is to get a T-shirt and fabric paint. Paint either on the front or the back the character trait word you're trying to add. On the opposite side write the definition. Wear the T-shirt as a reminder of the character trait you're working on.

Teens like doing this project and can come up with creative designs. They even like wearing them. If you don't want to go public with your character trait work, then you can write the character trait on a note card and carry it with you in your wallet or in your purse.

If you are put in a position that you think you will compromise and not exemplify the character trait you're working on, excuse yourself and go to the bathroom. Take the card out of your purse or wallet, read it out loud to reinforce your determination and resolve to add that trait to your product. Go back and face the temptation that challenged your resolve to compromise your work on YOU.

Although the above has been focused on developing good character traits, there are also ways to add more skills to your skill set or improve the ones you do have. Chapter 9 will go into greater detail explaining how you can do that.

Adding good character traits to your life is extremely important and is a process you should continue throughout your life. Warren Bennis, considered the father of leadership, said unequivocally that "Leadership is character," adding, *"It is not just a superficial question of style, but has to do with who we are as human beings, and with the forces that have shaped us. The process of becoming a leader is much the same as the process of becoming an integrated human being."*

Now that you see how important it is to manage your product well, let's go to the next step.

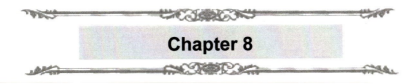

# Chapter 8

## Creating Your Own Distinct Brand

How do you want people to remember you? How do you want people to perceive you? That's what branding is about. When people think about you how would they describe you?

In business terms branding is the process of creating a unique name or image by which the customer will remember the company or its products or services. In your case the ultimate customer would be the prospective employer but it could also include your work peers and friends. Branding is about taking advantage of your points of difference to get the return you want, which would be a job or perhaps a promotion.

In business situations this may be the name, a term or symbol, or any unique element of the product or the company. There are some companies who have branded their products so well that you refer to the product by the company's name. Facial tissues are generally referred to as "Kleenex". "Jello" is another good example of branding. The Lexus and Mercedes logo emblems are an example of branding.

To more fully understand the concept of branding think of some companies who have done well branding their products or services. Branding **differentiates** you from others (your competitors). You can research companies online who have brilliantly differentiated themselves from their competition. See what they did and how they did it. Some that come to mind are Apple, Ben & Jerry's, and Burt's Bees.

You will have to begin to think in terms of how you can differentiate yourself from others who are applying for the job you want. Here are some questions you should consider. *What is unique about me that I can convey memorably to others? What is different about me? What is it that I can do that others can't? What are my marketable skills? Do I posses extraordinary or unusual experience? What have I accomplished?*

What is unique about you will sell you to the employer? To begin the process of creating your own distinct brand or image start by **making a list of the things about you that make you different and unique.**
Write down your professional skills and at least two points that would prove you have those skills. Also write down the experiences and character traits you have that will be an asset to a

company who hires you. As you add more professional skills, experiences and character traits to your life add them to the list.

Now begin to look at the things you listed and divide them into three categories: benefits, competencies and things that would give you a competitive advantage over another applicant for the same job. When companies create their brand or images they look at what they do and who they are from three different perspectives, which will be described below:

**Differential Benefit:** are the properties of a product or service that sets them apart from the competitors' products or service providing unique customer benefits. A benefit is how a product is "useful" to the customer. For example, Amazon is known as the company with the best customer service. Good customer service is their differential benefit. What will yours be? How will you be a benefit "useful" to the company that hires you? If you already know how to do the job, then if a company hired you they would not need to train you saving them time and money.

What is your differential benefit? Write it down.

**Competitive Advantage:** A competitive advantage is an advantage that a company has over its competitors. For example, Apple has used its technology innovations as a competitive advantage over other technology companies. A company gains a competitive advantage when it can outperform the competition. Competitive advantage can come to a company via product differentiation or operational efficiency.

What is your advantage over others who are in competition for the job?

Being a problem solver and having the ability to be a critical thinker can give you a competitive advantage over others applicants. You can outperform others by being a hard worker and not waste the company's time or money. Being a hard worker can help you outperform other employees. It may be your knowledge or experience in a specified field that will give you a competitive advantage.

Think about what advantages you have over others and write them down.

Distinct Competency: The distinctive competency of a firm refers to a set of activities or capabilities that a company is able to perform better than its competitors and which gives it an advantage over them. It is some superior capability that they have over the competition.

Capabilities are abilities. What superior ability do you have that others don't have?

Toyota has a distinct competency in the use of lean manufacturing. GE has a distinct competency in management development. For me it is the power of persuasion – passionate selling. Someone else may say it is adaptability - that no matter what situation is thrown at them, they can adapt.

Now that you have made your list and divided them into categories use these to create your brand. Remember branding is how you to set yourself apart from the competition. How do you want people to remember you.

## *Create your own personal brand*

Now hopefully, you begin to see that to create your "Brand" you consider these:

- How will you benefit a company? What about you makes you
  "useful" to a company? – **differential benefits.**
- What advantages do you have over others? –
  **competitive advantages.**
- What are your superior capabilities? – **distinct competencies.**

In 25 words or less, with around 150 characters, write your brand statement which conveys the image you want to portray to the world. Your brand statement should include your greatest marketable skills. The following are some examples:

Problem solver, vision creator, team builder, revenue generator, turn around expert, money saver, expert in operational efficiency and public speaker computer savvy, proactive seller, excellent with customer service, reliable employee and experienced traveler.

I energize, focus and align manufacturing organizations, resulting in sustainable acceleration of processes, reduction in waste, and growth of profits.

Write your brand statement using your skills, develop business cards (networking cards) with your picture on the front and your brand statement on the back. Begin to dress and act the part – appropriately display by your appearance and actions your brand image.

Check your online presence; see what has been said about you or what you've said about yourself with posts and pictures. Be sure your online brand image is the way you want people to perceive you, particularly a prospective employer. Later in Chapter 11 how to promote your brand will be discussed.

Hopefully you have noticed when you were listing your differential benefits, competitive advantages and distinct competencies, you were listing your strengths, professional skills, character traits, your abilities and competencies.

> *You are a Brand and a Good One at that!!!!*
> *Believe it!*

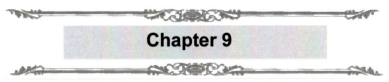

# Chapter 9

## The 2nd P of Marketing - Set the Right Price

Price is the value that is put on the product. The quality, image and/or benefits that a product offers make a difference about how much a consumer is willing to pay for the product.

So the quality and image that you portray and the benefits you can offer will help determine your price. This is why it is so important to brand yourself appropriately. YOU have the ability to determine what your price is. YOU determine your quality, YOU determine your image and YOU can offer benefits to a company via your education, skills, experience and character traits, which you can add to and improve.

You have both a professional and a personal price. The professional price is easier to understand as it relates to how much education you have, the experience you have and your marketable skills along with your character. But we have all seen people who excel professionally but their personal lives are a mess. Why is this?? It may be because their personal price is not high enough.

*You have a professional and a personal value.*

Let's look at how your price is determined professionally and personally.

Determining Your Professional Price:

Professionally your price is determined to a great extent by external factors. The qualifications required and preferred for a job and how well you meet those qualifications will determine your professional price (salary). The price you garner can be influenced by how many people apply for the job and what their education, experience and skills are.

The process of improving your professional price works something like this:

### 1. Determine your job objective
- What job do you want?
- Where do you want it to be (physical location)?

2. **Estimate the demand** (how many companies have job openings)

- Review newspaper ads, career websites and see how many job vacancies are listed for the job you want in the location you want to be in. Write down the job title, the company name along with the education, skills, experience required and salary ranges, if mentioned. When you finish your search you can then determine the demand (the number of job openings available).

- A friend I once carpooled to work with was constantly looking in the paper during our 45 minute commute When I asked him what he was doing, he said, "Looking for a job." I knew he had a good job so I said, "Why." He said, "I want a job at this hospital which is 20 minutes from where I want to live on my wife's family farm. I want to build a house there. I want to be prepared so that I am the one who gets the job." He eventually got everything he wanted.

3. **Determine the price**
- What are the salary ranges associated with the job openings that you found?

4. **Evaluate the environment**
- How much competition is there for these jobs?
- How many students are graduating from local universities with a degree in the same field you will be in?
- Will there be a major influx of people into the area because of plant openings or other business trends?
- Is the national and/or local economy good or bad? How will that affect the number of jobs that will be available in your field in the future?
- How is globalization and technology affecting the job field and the number of jobs in that field?

5. **Determine your price** (the salary you think you could get)
- What were the education, skills, and experience requirements for the jobs you found? List your educational achievements, your professional skills, your experience and work accomplishments.
- How does your education, your skills, and your experiences compare to the job requirements?
- Now estimate what you are worth compared to the salary ranges you found for the job openings?

Remember no job is worth the salary, if you hate it.

Once you have done these things, you can estimate what you are worth professionally. "Create a list of specific skills and knowledge you should develop to improve your value. Below are some suggestions on how to do that:

- take courses that relate to the educational requirements or
  courses that enhance your knowledge
- obtain specific certifications
- obtain an internship
- look for an apprenticeship
- look for volunteering opportunities
- look for strategic moonlighting opportunities.

*Develop a strategy to improve your value.*

## Determining Your Personal Price

Now you know how to determine or estimate your professional price BUT what does personal price mean?

*Your personal value is determined by*
*how you respond to the way people treat you.*

Some people are treated with respect and consideration. Others are berated, fussed at, talked down to and even hit and beaten. Which category do you fit into? Or maybe you're somewhere in between. Unfortunately, some people have been so demeaned that they do not realize how mistreated they are.

When someone asks me how to make people see that they are being mistreated, my only suggestion is to ask them who they love the most – a parent, a child, a best friend or a pet? Then ask them if someone were hitting, beating or mean to the person or animal they love, would that be right?

For those who have been abused or controlled for a long time they may be so conditioned they don't respond to the abuse or control; they acquiesce to it. It is as though they are emotionally numb and thus, incapable of taking action. They may even assume responsibility for the mistreatment; somehow they feel they did something wrong and it is their fault. When this happens this takes the abuser off the hook and they have no responsibility for their actions. Often women who are abused will go back time and time again to the abuser. Don't allow this situation in your life!

**YOU** are entirely responsible for your personal value. It may be because of your inaction that other people assign low value to you as a human being.

Dr. Phillip C. McGraw says, "You teach people how to treat you or how to continue to treat you – by the way you respond." (Relationship Rescue, page 37) This is very true!

> *How you allow people to treat you is related to how you feel, value, and respect yourself and how others feel, value and respect you.*

You can allow your personal value to be determined by outside factors. When someone says, "You are no good and won't ever amount to anything," and you believe it; you have assigned a low value to yourself. When you believe those negative things you hear other people say about you or to you and base your value on what they say, you are allowing others to set your value.

If you allow others to set your personal value low you put yourself in the bargain basement or in a disorganized, poorly lit, cheap discount store. If we think we are not attractive, are too heavy because of media advertisements or celebrities, we have allowed others to set our price.

If on the other hand, you think that your product is based on what you know about yourself, those positive words you used to describe yourself earlier, then you will begin to see that you are valuable. As you continue to add good character traits, more skills and recognize your distinct competencies, differential benefits and competitive advantages, you should begin to think of yourself as a good and valuable product. You should be respected. You do have the right to express your feelings. You should feel that you are entitled to have "Every Human Being's Bill of Rights." (See Chapter 6). It says "EVERY" Human Being's Bill of Rights."

Are you being treated like a trash can or a treasure chest? How have you set your personal value?

*You set your value by how you respond to the way other people to treat you.*

Set boundaries for your life. A good place to start is with the "Every Human Being's Bill of Rights." Also read the book, "Boundaries" by Henry Cloud and John Townsend. Make a list of your boundaries. If you don't set boundaries you have set a low value on yourself personally.

Allow people to treat you according to the boundaries you have set for your life. If you do set boundaries and don't allow people to violate those boundaries, you have established a high value for your product.

Boundaries are like property lines. If you own land that land is defined legally by the property lines. The land owner can determine who can and who cannot come on their property. The owner can also determine what can and cannot be done to their property.

For example, if you allow someone to hit you more than once, you have not established a boundary. Your boundaries are determined by how you respond to what people say and do to you. For example, if your sister yells at you over the phone and says mean and hateful things to you, if you truly believe you have rights, you can quietly and calmly say, "I choose not to listen to this and I am hanging up the phone". You have just assigned a value to yourself and it is one of worth. When you realize that you are valuable, you can make that evident to the people in your life.

There are situations that are dangerous or you cannot afford to stand up for your rights. You have to consider those situations and the cost of standing up. In those situations you need to develop a plan to ultimately remove yourself from the situation. The statement below is crucial to learning how to get out of a situation and how to control your emotions in order to make good decisions.

*You can not change another person. The only person you can change is YOU.*

39

One of the first things you must realize is that you can not change or control another person.  The only person you can change or control is YOU.  To enforce your boundaries may mean leaving the situation or strategizing so that you can eventually leave the situation.

> *You raise your price by believing*
> *in your product, YOU!*

How do you believe in your product, YOU, and how do you raise your price?

1.  Continue to list the good things you like about yourself.

2.  Practice the 10 Steps to Self-Esteem (Chapter 6)

3.  Believe in Your Bill of Rights as a human being and appropriately respond when one of your rights has been violated. (See Every Human Being's Bill of Rights – Chapter 6)

4.  Read the suggested books listed at the end of this book, especially "Boundaries."

5.  Continually keep the vision you have for your life before you and don't let anyone destroy that vision.

6.  Believe that you were born with natural abilities and talents which make you unique and equip you to succeed.

7.  And thus, you should believe that there is a good plan for your life which is good and not evil, which should always give you hope for the end that you expect.

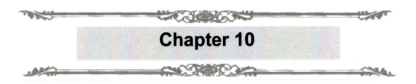

# Chapter 10

## The 3rd P in Marketing – Being in the Right Places

In marketing, place refers to where you make the product available for the customer. It is the channel or route used to get you to your destination.

How does place relate to marketing yourself?

The place (location) today has gotten much more complex than it was previously. Place would refer to where you can be to get the attention of the employers you're interested in getting a job with.

By the time you're interested in determining the places to be to get attention, you have worked on getting your product prepared for the marketplace. You have worked on the educational requirements, honed your skill set, worked to get experience, are continually developing your character traits and have worked on your weaknesses. Now you are ready to put yourself out there to be noticed.

Since most people use the **internet** now, including employers and career websites, this is the first place you need to go. You will need a GOOD presence on the internet. First review what is already out there about you. Hopefully, it is nothing bad. If it is bad then you will need to work on getting that removed. Hopefully it will not take your employing a lawyer to do so. Remember the character trait, "live above reproach." Now you should understand why that trait was listed first in the list of character traits to acquire. (See Chapter 7) Prospective employers DO look at your Facebook page. Carefully consider what you put on there.

You will need to post your resume on the top career websites making sure that you've included words that describe the key skills and qualifications you have for the job you're applying for. The prospective employer might also have a website that accepts applications.

Establish a robust presence on the internet. Set up a LinkedIn account. You might also want to create a website that showcases your experience, skills and education. Having a video resume that showcases your skills and personality would be a plus, if you're comfortable doing that. Getting endorsements, recommendations or testimonials about you on your website or on LinkedIn would be good. Keep your contact information current and easy to access.

You've heard that it's not what you know but who you know that gets you a job. A study by Mark Granoveter proved that but his findings were interesting. He found that people were 58% more likely to get a new job through weak ties than strong ties, meaning that acquaintances can be more helpful than good friends. That makes **networking** EXTREMELY important for you to do. Thus, I would strongly suggest you join professional organizations related to your field. There are accounting professional organizations, advertising ones and logistics and supply chain, just to mention a few. Take your networking card to the meetings.

Look for opportunities to volunteer with community service organizations. There are many not-for-profit organizations which always need help. The more you get out and about the more people you will meet. You might want to look at the Volunteer Match Organization website for volunteer opportunities in your area. This site also has Board Development opportunities via city. The more you are out in the community the more people you will meet.

You **can** also put yourself in the right places to gain experience or to improve your skills. Join Toastmasters, if you have a fear of public speaking. You can ask to volunteer at the company you are most interested in working for. That's an "outside the box" idea. Think of other ones.

**Not** putting yourself *in the wrong places* where people may perceive that you are not a good product is just as important; like frequenting bars, night clubs, and strip clubs. I once had a boss who would check out a prospective employee's standing in the community before he hired them. He believed that if a person had a good standing in the community they would be a good employee for him. He was correct. He has now become the President and CEO of a large healthcare system in a major city in Texas. The lesson here is for you to be one of those good people who an employer would want to hire.

You can be in the right place at the right time but if you're not a good product it won't matter.

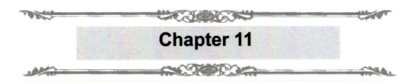

# Chapter 11

## The 4th P of Marketing – Promoting Yourself Effectively

Promotion in marketing is the coordination of a marketer's *communications efforts* to influence attitudes or behavior in order to inform or persuade consumers to purchase products.

So when you think about promoting yourself, promotions are all the ways that you will communicate your "brand" image to other people.  Are you promoting yourself in the ways that you would like?

Are you promoting yourself in a professional, personable way or are you promoting yourself in a non-professional, non-personable way?  Are your communications going to be effective?  Will they influence the attitudes and behaviors of others so that they are informed and persuaded that you are a valuable product – both professionally and personally?

You communicate in a lot of different ways – verbally, in writing, or physically: your body language, personality, appearance, and how you dress.

> *Your total product package should be one that communicates "I am valuable and I will be a benefit to you."*

When marketers communicate they do it by delivering a message. So likewise, you should also have a message.  Your message should have the intent that it will inform or persuade someone that you bring value to the table.  Remember your brand statement that you created earlier.

How do you create your message?

To deliver an effective message you must know your audience. Is it a job interviewer, your boss, a colleague or someone else?

Once you have identified the audience try to determine who they are, what they want and how you can convince them that you can fill the bill.

If you have been working through this book and not just reading it, you have listed your strengths, the things you like about yourself. You have listed your skills, your educational accomplishments and your experiences (accomplishments). This is where you pull your list of values and benefits that you can bring to your audience to meet their needs.

Now develop your narrative or your story about what you can do, what you have done and how you can benefit them. People like stories, if they are not too long.

With the above concepts in mind think about how you will create your message via your resume so that the person looking at it quickly gets what you can do for them. How about listing your competencies right across the top with bulleted points? Competencies or benefits are how you can specifically be useful to a company. Look back at your brand statement for ideas. The remainder of the resume will have to prove you can do those things. You should list your "accomplishments" not just what you did but what you accomplished; i.e., saved the company $1 ml.

How will you deliver your message on LinkedIn, on your website, with a video? Promoting yourself is about delivering an impactful message that will be memorable.

You can advertise yourself by posting your resume on career websites, creating a LinkedIn account, develop a personal website. These are written promotions. Some people have even created personal promotional videos for jobs and posted these online. They have videotaped themselves telling about who they are from a professional standpoint.

Your sales promotions can be attending job fairs, social events, volunteering and joining professional organizations. Assuming a leadership position in a professional organization is a good promotional tool and can give you new skills. If you enjoy public speaking look for opportunities to do that. The more you speak the more comfortable you will be doing it.

Always have your networking card with you to hand out. You don't have to have a job to have a "business" card.

You can create one with your name and contact information and picture on the front and your "Brand Me" statement on the back.

*Network, network, network!*

Don't forget your body language. That is also a promotional tool and can speak volumes about who you are. A good video to watch is Amy Cuddy's TED talk on "Your body language shapes who you are." When you walk out of the house how you dress conveys a message. What if you were going to meet someone who could give you a job? Would you dress differently?

You are delivering a promotional message about who you are and what value you bring every time you write anything, every time you speak, when you walk out of the house or when you post anything online. Positive and upbeat messages are the best. You may not be naturally upbeat or positive or you may be shy or introverted BUT there is nothing about you that YOU cannot change. The most effective promotion communications are upbeat and positive. Don't brag – inform and smile.

In my past, I was a not a positive person and by all rights had justification for not being positive. But I came to a particularly difficult juncture where I had to leave a house I had spent 3 years remodeling just at the time when I could have begun to enjoy it. I had to move to Atlanta for a job and the daffodils that we had planted by flashlight one cold November night had bloom buds appearing. I didn't know when or if I would ever see them bloom.

Although this might be considered an insignificant event for some, Three years and a cold November night wasn't insignificant at the time. When I got to Atlanta all of a sudden I realized that I could either be miserable every day in Atlanta or make a decision to enjoy everyday there. I made the decision to enjoy it and when it came time for me to move back to Alabama, I didn't want to move. I realized from that experience that being positive is a choice.

Choose everyday to be positive, even if it means putting a positive (+) or negative (–) sign on the bathroom mirror to remind you every morning that you have a choice each day whether you will be positive or negative.

Public relations and personal selling are things you do everyday by the way you dress, carry yourself, display your personality and interact with people. How are you doing in these areas? If you are negative, that comes through. If you cannot control your emotions, that is evident. Watch how large companies conduct their public relations efforts and take lessons from them. Companies send out press releases when they have done something good. They do something good and then they tell you about it. When a catastrophic event occurs they manage it with a calm, collected and informative public relations strategy.

Be careful that your collective communications efforts, whether verbal, written or physical, are continuingly sending the right message – I *am a good product with value and worth and will be a benefit for you. I am different and unique.* You only have one chance to make a good first impression. Be prepared everyday by how you dress, what you say and how you conduct yourself to meet the person who might give you a job. You never know! You want people to remember that you possess skills and abilities that no one else does. Promoting yourself comes from finding a compelling way to tell (communicate) the story about your differences and uniqueness and how they will be a benefit (useful).

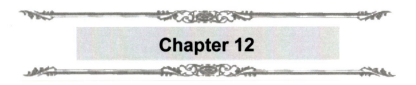

# Chapter 12

## "Success Builders"
## Things that make you more marketable

In marketing, the process of making a product more marketable is called continuous product improvement.

To make your product, YOU, more marketable you should continuously be aware of the ways that you can improve yourself. It should be a lifelong process. It is not about competing with someone else. It is about you competing with yourself, making yourself better. Make it an enjoyable lifelong process of learning, because that's what it really is.

*There are 5 areas to focus on when considering continuous product improvement of your product, YOU. These areas are appearance, communication skills, education, finances, manners and appreciation of the arts.*

Improving in these 5 areas can make you more marketable.

1. **Appearance** – is about looking as attractive as You can by dressing appropriately, eating right, exercising and making the most of your physical attributes. It's about making a good first impression.

   We are all different shapes and sizes, different ages and genders. That is what makes us unique. And our uniqueness makes the world a more interesting place. We should not obsess about our appearance. Nor should we let the media dictate what we should look like. Unless we have a personal hair dresser, personal wardrobe consultant, a personal trainer and a personal airbrush artist, we can't look perfect. Let's get over it and make the most of what we have.

   Appearance includes:
   - **Dress**
     Dressing appropriately pertains to knowing how to emphasize the attractive points about your body shape

and size and how to de-emphasize those that may not be as attractive. Clothes today seem to be made in one style only and everyone, regardless of size and shape, is supposed to look good in them. Unfortunately, this is not the case.

As a home economics major I learned how to make the most of my body shape and size by choosing the right styles, lengths, and fabric patterns. It is a fact that we are different and we can make the most of what we have. The TV show, "What Not to Wear" exemplifies those basic clothing principles that I learned in home economics classes.

The major keys to successful dressing are to:

1. Package yourself for where you want to be not for where you are now.

2. Select clothes that accentuate your positive body features and deemphasize the negative ones.

3. Don't spend a fortune on fads. Spend more on classic clothes that you can wear longer.

4. Take care of the clothes you do have. Washing it in the washer may be OK but hang it on a hanger to dry. Hand washing an item may be better.

5. Dress appropriately for the occasion. It is better to dress up than down.

6. Be a role model for others in the way you dress. If you teach school, show students how to dress by what you wear. Do not dress like the students.

7. Don't deface your body with tattoos and piercings. This may be a controversial statement but you never want to wear anything where people's focus gravitates to any one thing and not on the person as a whole. I learned this principle when designing room interiors. You want to create interiors so that people walk in and say what beautiful room. The focus should not be on any one item.

- **Eating**

Eating correctly as an adult is about eating:
1. 2 fruits a day
2. 5 vegetables a day
3. 8 glasses of water a day
4. fiber each day – whole grain cereals, bread, pasta, etc.
5. milk and dairy products for calcium
6. 1 – 2 lean meats per day (chicken, turkey, beef and pork) in small
   portions – fish, eggs, legumes, nuts, etc.
7. appropriate portions for your size and activity levels

This is just a basic quick, simple guide. You should obtain more information from recognized nutritional sources.

Please do not buy into the advertisements about diets. Eating healthy is about eating right. Academic studies have shown that our present obsession with appearance and thinness has been fueled by companies who wanted to make money selling diet foods, pills, and books about dieting. Why would you want to jeopardize your health so someone else can make money?

Remember that marketing promotions are about a marketer's communications efforts to influence attitudes or behavior in order to inform or persuade consumers to purchase products, even diet products.

- **Exercise**

The basic thing to remember about exercise is that a balanced exercise program consists of three types of work- outs: a cardiovascular workout, strength training, and stretching for balance and flexibility.

Exercise at least 30 minutes per day, 5-6 days a week. Being active will help your body stay strong and healthy.

## 2. Good Communication Skills

Good communication skills involve being able to speak using correct pronunciation and avoiding colloquial expressions. Writing correctly involves using correct grammar and punctuation and being able to organize your material in such a manner that the reader quickly and clearly understands what you are trying to communicate. Good communication skills help you develop and maintain relationships whether they are professional or personal.

## 3. Education/Learning

Education is a critical component of product improvement.

An education empowers you to:
- get a better job and have a better life
- get out of difficult situations
- become independent and not dependent on someone
- feel better about yourself

A major component of education is not just going to school and getting a high school diploma, a bachelor's degree, master's degree or even a doctoral degree. Education can come from getting certifications and different experiences and choosing to be a lifelong learner. Learning can be fun and you can love to learn by taking courses from great teachers who are enthusiastic about what they teach.

Continuous learning:
- makes you more interesting
- makes you more valuable to an employer
- enriches your life and makes it more fun
- is exciting
- makes you qualified for more jobs
- enlarges your perspective of the world and life
- makes you less judgmental, prejudiced and critical
- makes you more self-confident

*Never stop learning.*

One person I know in their list of values states: "To learn something new personally and professionally each day."

You can learn by reading books. Remember CEOs of companies read over 35 books a year. How many books are you reading? You might have to stop watching TV, playing video games, or being on Facebook but its' important to set a book reading goal each year.

## 4. Good Financial Practices

Every successful company has a budget and you need to
develop a budget with financial objectives that will help you
reach your vision.

A budget starts with your earnings. From that you subtract
your monthly expenses like house payments (rent), food,
utility bills, car payments, insurance, etc. What is left after
subtracting for things you have to have is known as your
discretionary income, money that is not set aside for
something else but can be spent on things you want.

**First**, take out at least 10% of your net income and invest it
in an account where you will earn interest. This should be
done before you spend any of your discretionary income on
things you want. I recommend that you save between
10 – 20% from each paycheck.
**Pay yourself first.**

At the end of this book you will find suggested books to
read on good financial practices.  NEVER spend more than
you make and don't put anything on a credit card that you
can't pay off when the bill comes due.

## 5. Good Manners and Appreciating the Arts

To make your product polished and one of excellence,
learn good manners and develop an appreciation for the
fine arts – art, the symphony, ballet, opera, theater.

On my 16th birthday my mother gave me Emily Post's Book
on Etiquette and I was expected to read it in its entirety.  I
was required to learn everything in it and use.  I did what
she said and I was never in any social situation where I
didn't know how to eat appropriately, how to introduce
someone, or what to wear.

*These success builders are attributes that will*
*polish/refine your product and raise your value.*

When marketers want to create the image of a luxury product they will package it in black with gold lettering, put it in a velvet  bag or use expensive woods and elegant furnishings to create an atmosphere of wealth. These are things that marketers do to establish that a product is a prestige product. Good manners and an appreciation of the arts –opera, ballet, theater, the symphony, and art- can put you in the prestige product category. It increases your value and worth.

Review all the success builders and resolve to add these to your product. You won't be sorry you did.

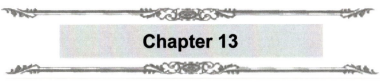

# Chapter 13

## "Success Busters"
## Avoiding things that make you unmarketable

**Definition:** A "Success Buster," is anything that will make you unmarketable or less marketable. It is anything that will physically or emotionally harm you, make your life harder, make it take longer for you to reach your vision or keep you from your vision altogether.

**My definition of an addiction** continually doing something even when it will destroy you physically or financially. Any addiction is a success buster.

The success busters are listed below with a brief explanation of each. Success buster # 3 will be discussed in detail in the next chapter.

**Success Buster # 1: Body or Brain Killers** – drugs, alcohol, sexual addiction, smoking, eating disorders, self-mutilation, anorexia/bulimia.

**Success Buster # 2: Other Addictions** – wanting the approval of others, spending.

**Success Buster # 3: Poor financial management.**
Spending more than you make and not saving a percentage of your income consistently.

**Success Buster # 4: Uncontrolled Emotions:** Fear, Self-Pity, Negativity, Worry, Worthlessness, Anger and Laziness.

**Success Buster # 5:** Yielding to Peer Pressure, Making Wrong Choices, Letting your Life be Ruined by Bad Relationships

**Success Buster # 6: Other** - posting things on the Internet that will make you look bad, doing something (bad behavior) that is reported on the Internet, not being able to verbally communicate well, not dressing appropriately. Let's just face it, there are times you HAVE to conform in dress and behavior to succeed. Conforming is not compromising values.

> *Stay far away from the success busters.*
> *They can **destroy** your happiness and your life.*
> *They can ruin your success and **keep you from**
> **attaining your vision.***
> *They can leave you destitute and/or dead.*

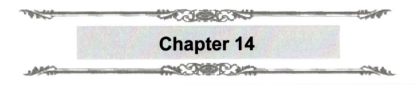

# Chapter 14

## Emotions a Major "Success Buster"

Definition of Emotions: strong feelings that are the results of either pain or pleasure which can cause you to react and move in a certain direction that is either negative or positive.

If you can control your emotions instead of letting them control you, your decision making skills will not be impaired by your emotions. This allows you to make better decisions. Success in life is about making good decisions.

- Just as a car battery has a positive and negative charge, your brain is charged by positive or negative thoughts. You will have positive or negative emotions because of those thoughts.

- Therefore, your thoughts control your emotions and your emotions influence your actions.

- The root of negative emotions is a sense of powerlessness over your ability to change yourself, another person, a situation or circumstances.

- It is not psychologically healthy to deny that you have feelings and emotions. However, you don't have to let them control you or the actions you take.

- When you learn to control your thoughts you can control your emotions.

- People may try to manipulate and/or control you by trying to play with your emotions. They may use guilt, anger, or manipulate you by being really nice in order to get something from you or get you to let them do something.

- Negative emotions are: fear, self-pity, depression, anger, worry, feelings of worthlessness, guilt, oneliness, and sadness.  Negative feelings make you feel hopeless, make you feel like a victim and out of control.

• Positive emotions are: joy, happiness, peace, love, self-control, self-worth, contentment.  Positive feelings make you feel hopeful and in control.

• Using alcohol, drugs or looking at pornographic images will make your emotions uncontrollable.  Alcohol is a depressant and can also drastically affect your actions.

• Signs that you need help dealing with emotions and negative feelings include gaining or losing excessive weight without trying, turning to alcohol or drugs, or feeling hopeless and being emotionally out of control.

• Thinking about suicide or other violent acts are also danger signs.  Get Help!!  If you notice these signs, talk with a trusted friend, family member, counselor or health care provider. The most important step to feeling better is asking for help!

• Use the 7 Steps to Problem Solving to help you deal with your negative feelings and change your thinking. (See Below)

**You cannot change or control another person.**
BUT you can change yourself and how you react.
You can develop a plan to get away from the
person or out of the situation that is causing
difficulty and hardships in your life.

**Do what you can do about a situation, but don't worry
about the things you can't do anything about.**

• Replace negative thoughts with **positive** ones:

| Negative Thoughts | Positive Thoughts |
|---|---|
| Fear | Faith |
| Hopelessness | Hope |
| Anger, Getting Mad | Self-control |
| Worry | Trust |
| Depression | Choose Happiness |

- It takes hard work and practice to replace negative thoughts with positive ones.  Don't hang around people who are negative.  You will be influenced by their negativity and you will begin doing the same thing.  You'll think negatively, talk negatively and it will affect your actions.

- Find a friend who is willing to practice positive thinking and speaking with you.  Make a game of it by correcting each other when you say something negative;  think of something positive to say instead.  Eventually you can think positively without stopping and forcing yourself to speak that way.

- Speaking positive things is very important. Your negative thoughts change faster to positive ones when you hear yourself saying positive things.  You will have to practice thinking and speaking positively. Your mind is where the battle takes place. Be determined to win.

- When you begin to feel upset, anxious, uneasy, or nervous about a situation, circumstance or decision, that is an indication that you are being influenced or controlled by your emotions.  STOP!!  and rethink the issue.

- Remember that you cannot change or control another person. The only thing you can do is change yourself and control yourself. Make a decision to change you or your circumstances.

*Make a decision that you will NOT let emotions control or master your life, and you will NOT make emotional decisions.*

Below are listed 7 steps that you can learn which will help you solve problems or make decisions. Learn and practice these steps. The more you practice them the better you will be. You will be able to face a problem or a decision and automatically apply these steps without having your emotions cloud the issues. This is a great empowering tool. Learn the steps and use them.

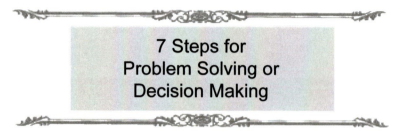

# 7 Steps for Problem Solving or Decision Making

**Step 1: Identify the Problem (Problem Recognition) Define the Decision to be made.**
- A problem is a situation where the existing state is NOT the desired state.
- "You can't change what you don't acknowledge." Dr. Phillip McGraw Life Strategies, page 109.
- Call it what it is: verbal abuse, physical abuse, lack of money, etc.
- Define what the decision is that you have to make

**Step 2: Look at What You Can Change and What You Cannot Change**
- You cannot change what another person does or says.
- You can change how you think and react to what another person says or does.
- You can change yourself.
- You usually can change all or part of a situation, maybe not immediately but eventually.
- Ask for advice from wise, trustworthy people and listen!

**Step 3: Search for Information on Possible Solutions for the Problem or for the Information Needed to Make the Best Decision**
- Do research on the Internet
- Read books

- Talk to a trusted counselor, official, or professional, or someone with expertise on your problem, or who has experience that will help you make the best decision.

**Step 4: Evaluate the Alternatives (Solutions) that will Eliminate the Problem or Lessen (Reduce) its Impact. Evaluate the Alternative Choices for \ Decisions**
- List all the possible solutions for a problem and all the alternative choices for decisions.
- List under each the advantages and disadvantages of using that solution or making each choice
- List what resources it will take (money, education, other people's help, etc.) to implement each solution or to make each choice.

**Step 5: Pick the Best Solution or Choice**

**Step 6: Implement the Solution (Start Working the Solution) or Choice**

**Step 7: Evaluate the Effectiveness of the Solution or Choice and if necessary, change or alter the solution or choice to achieve the results you set out to accomplish.**

*Letting Your Emotions take over your thinking on any one of the steps will negatively affect your problem solving skills and your logical and rational decision making skills.*
*It Will Knock You Off Any of These Steps?*

**When you let your emotions take over you stop thinking rationally and logically.**

**"The most important person you will have to learn to manage is yourself."** Robert Steven Kaplan

The 7 Steps to Problem Solving or

Developing Coping Skills

WHAT WILL KNOCK YOU
OFF THESE STEPS?

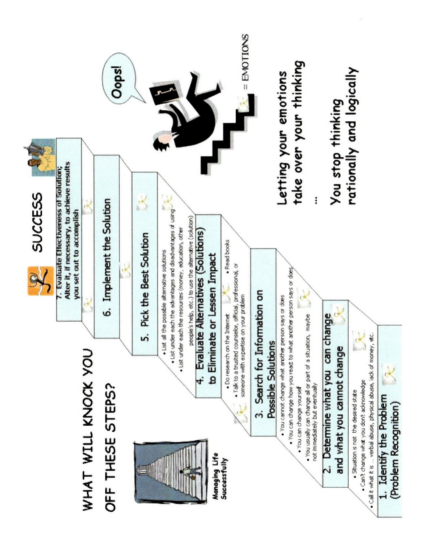

Managing Life
Successfully

SUCCESS

7. Evaluate Effectiveness of Solution;
Alter it, if necessary, to achieve results
you set out to accomplish

6. Implement the Solution

5. Pick the Best Solution

• List all the possible alternative solutions
• List under each the advantages and disadvantages of using
• List under each the resources (money, education, other
  people's help, etc.) to use the alternative (solution)

4. Evaluate Alternatives (Solutions)
to Eliminate or Lessen Impact

• Do research on the Internet          • Read books
• Talk to a trusted counselor, official, professional, or
  someone with expertise on your problem

3. Search for Information on
Possible Solutions

• You cannot change what another person says or does
• You can change how you react to what another person says or does
• You can change yourself
• You usually can change all or part of a situation,  maybe
  not immediately but eventually

2. Determine what you  can change
and what you cannot change

• Situation is not  the desired state
• Can't change what you don't acknowledge
• Call it what it is ... verbal abuse, physical abuse, lack of money, etc.

1. Identify the Problem
(Problem Recognition)

Oops!

= EMOTIONS

Letting your emotions
take over your thinking
...

You stop thinking
rationally and logically

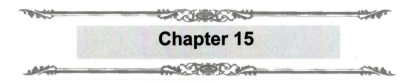

# Chapter 15

## Relationship Deal Breakers

Definition:  A relationship deal breaker is something that when it occurs in a relationship the relationship should automatically be over.  **There is no discussion, no ifs, no ands, and no buts. It's over!!**

Why would there be a section about relationship deal breakers?  Some of you don't like yourselves, you don't feel you have value or self-worth because of what someone did to you or said about you.  Some of you are afraid because of the dysfunctional environments you live in and you are constantly in emotional turmoil.  Had you realized that these people or situations caused you to devalue yourself perhaps you might have seen that they were the problem and not you.  Now that you know you are valuable and have self-esteem, you don't need to subject yourself to people or situations that will destroy you physically, emotionally or financially.

When people makes excuses for people who do bad things because they had a bad family life, or they were mistreated as a child; etc., I have a saying,

*"There is never a good excuse for bad behavior."*

So when you see the situations listed below in others who are in your life, I strongly feel that they are a relationship "deal breaker." They are:

- Use of drugs or alcohol.
  (Comment:  You may feel that this statement regarding alcohol is too rigid.  However, I have personally witnessed the destructive power of alcohol in two different families.  The effects have been passing from generation to generation [parents to children and even to grandchildren].  In those two families 16 people's lives were either destroyed or severely damaged. No one can predict that they will

become an alcoholic when they take that first drink. too high. Don't do it.)

- Watching pornography (of any kind), going to strip clubs, massage parlors  or using escort services.

- Physical abuse:  hitting, beating, slapping, pushing, etc.

- Emotional abuse, verbal abuse, cursing: When someone says or does anything that makes another person feel worthless and disrespected. When someone violates your "Every Human Being's Bill of Rights" (See Chapter 6)

- Excessive spending that jeopardizes your financial well-being. This is being a spendaholic.

- Controlling what you do, where you go, who you see and how you live your life.

- Insisting you do something that YOU DON'T WANT TO DO and when you say "NO" the other person gets mad, makes you feel guilty, or tries to manipulate you into doing it by making you think they won't like you.

- When a person cannot be trusted.  Trust is the cornerstone to any good relationship.

### *These are deal breakers*

If you are in a situation were there is a deal breaker and cannot immediately leave, make a plan whereby you can eventually leave.
If you are in physical danger you will need to leave immediately and seek help from someone or an agency.

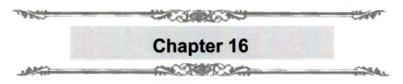

# Chapter 16

## The Even Dozen Keys to Success

**1. Feel good about yourself.** This is the first and most important key to being successful. You must do what it takes to develop self-esteem. Start listing the good things about yourself. You can never relate to people in a non-defensive or non- judgmental way until you first like yourself and feel secure in who you are.

**2. Work hard.** Be the best you can be. Never look at others to compete with them, compete only with yourself, getting better and better every day. My daddy, Bryan Simmons McLemore taught me, "If you are a ditch digger be the best ditch digger you can be."

**3. Network** – Relationships are crucial to success. Develop as many relationships as you can. Remember it's not just your friends who can help you but more likely, it will be an acquaintance.

**4. Value people.** Regardless of their physical appearance, race or socio-economic status, almost everyone can contribute something to your life or impart some knowledge you don't have. I have found that the most loyal, giving people are those who may be physically unattractive or who don't have a lot of money.

**5. Never give up or quit.** All of us at sometime or other in our lives will get knocked down or have some extraordinary difficulties. Believe that what appears to "be a long time is just temporary" and that **there is a good plan for your life.**

**6. Give it the "newspaper" or "internet" test.** If you would be embarrassed or ashamed if it appeared on the front page of the newspaper or was forever available online, DON'T DO IT. This is why you need to "live above reproach" all the time, every day.

**7. Learn to laugh.** Find something humorous even about difficult situations and learn to laugh at yourself. Be positive and joyful. It's a choice.

**8. Face fears.** Fear can make you lose focus, emotionally compromise you and can ultimately debilitate you. Face fears head on until you conquer them. Do it afraid!

**9. Let go of bad relationships.** When people don't help you grow, don't respect you or themselves, create difficult situations for you, or don't allow you to have rights and boundaries for yourself, let them go. Don't hang on.

**10. Learn how to negotiate.** Everyone wants something and when you learn what they want, you should be able to negotiate a win – win situation for both you and them.

**11. Never stop learning.** Be interested in new things, new ideas, and new information. Knowledge is power and it can change your life, if you use it. Read, read, read, read!

**12. Be someone who can be loved and respected** for your honesty, integrity and fairness for this perhaps is the greatest indicator that you are successful. Be a person with good character.

# Chapter 17

## How You Know You Are Empowered to Succeed?

- When you believe in yourself and have established boundaries for your life.

- When you can respect others and their boundaries. When you can work well together in a team.

- When you are willing to work hard to be the best you can be and you continue this process forever.

- When you chose to be positive rather than negative.

- When you are living above reproach: not doing anything that would embarrasses yourself, your family or your friends.

- When you can let go of a bad relationship.

- When you have learned how "not" to be ruled by emotions.

- When you are continuously learning and improving yourself. When you realize that reading books is important.

- When you're making progress toward your vision.

Now that you know how to market yourself successfully. GET WITH IT!

Practice what you've learned in this book and do it even if you are afraid to do it or you think it is hard to do. It will be worth it!

*You can be successful and you can change your circumstances by changing YOU, believing in YOU and taking care of YOURSELF!!!*

In Appendix A there is a marketing plan template. You might want to take this template and complete your own Personal Marketing Plan taking in consideration all that you have learned from this book. It can serve as the plan for you to achieve the vision you have for your life.

# Suggested Reading

1. **Boundaries** by Henry Cloud and John Townsend

2. **Self Matters** by Phillip C. McGraw

3. **Approval Addiction** by Joyce Meyer

4. **The Confident Woman** by Joyce Meyer

5. **Life Strategies** by Phillip C. McGraw

## Manage Your Product

1. **Talent is Never Enough** by John Maxwell

2. **The 7 Habits of Highly Effective People**
   by Stephen R. Covey

3. **How to Win Friends and Influence People**
   by Dale Carnegie

4. **The Power of Positive Thinking** by Norman Vincent Peal

5. **Enthusiasm Makes the Difference**
   by Norman Vincent Peal

6. **Reinventing You: Define Your Brand, Imagine Your Future**
   by Dorie Clark

7. **What You're Really Meant To Do** by Robert Steven Kaplan

## Make Yourself More Marketable – Success Builders

1. **The Total Money Makeover** by Dave Ramsey

2. **Emily Post's Etiquette**, 17th edition by Peggy Post

3. **25 Ways to Win with People** by John Maxwell

4. **The Wall Street Journal** – a business newspaper

5. **Use What You've Got** by Barbara Corcoran


## Avoiding Things that Make You Unmarketable

1. **How to Stop Worrying and Start Living** by Dale Carnegie

## Relationship Deal Breakers

1. **Relationship Rescue** by Phillip C. McGraw

2. **Safe People** by Henry Cloud and John Townsend

## Marketing Plan Template

1. **Executive Overview**  (The objective of this section is for the reader to know who you are and what you want to achieve.) It is a brief summary of who you are.  It includes answers to questions like: Where were you born?  Where did you go to school? Do you work and what do you do? Do you have a family?  What are your passions?  What do you want to ultimately do?  What are your hobbies?  Be brief make it no longer than 1/4 - 1/3 of a page.

2. **Vision Statement**  - is a statement of what you want to become and what you want to have.

3. **Mission Statement** – is a statement of your purpose. In addition your values should be included in this section to serve as the guardrails of your life.  They should serve as your moral compass.

4. **External Situation Analysis** – is an evaluation of the external environment in which you will live and work. In this section you should look at the health of the overall economy in the U.S. and globally.  You should research the industry you plan to seek a career in to evaluate the growth potential for that industry. Then you should evaluate the growth potential for your specific job choice. Will there be job growth or will globalization and technology changes affect the number and types of jobs?  What is your competition going to be? Is the job field teaming with lots of job applicants?

5. **Internal Situation Analysis** – is your identification of your strengths and weaknesses. To identify your strengths begin by creating a list of the good things you like about yourself, your  skills (good writer, etc.) and your good character traits. Then make a list of your weaknesses, such as procrastination, being shy, poor time management, etc. Strengths are really what you're capable of doing. Your good character traits and weaknesses are what you feel you have issues with or don't have skills in.

6. **SWOT Analysis** – is your identification, after you've done both the external and internal situation analysis, of what your strengths, weaknesses and the threats you face and the opportunities you have. With your education, skills and the economic environment for the job you want how do you measure up and will you be able to get a job?

If you can get a job what salary do you think you will have based on your education, skills and experience?

What will you have to do to obtain the necessary education or certifications? Will you need more experience and/or more skills? What will you do to eliminate your weaknesses? How will you promote yourself, where and what will your message be? These are all the things you will need to consider to develop your goals, which are discussed next. Think about these goals in terms of product improvement. Then think about promotional goals. How will you promote yourself? You are developing a marketing plan for you.

Note: If you are really serious about managing your life well and achieving your vision, there are two books that will help you develop an outstanding marketing plan. "One is Reinventing You" by Dorie Clark and the other is "What You're Really Meant To Do" by Robert Steven Kaplan.

7. **Goals** – are the milestones you want to achieve in order to reach your vision. Goals should be written in SMART terms. **S**pecific, **M**easurable, **A**ttainable, **R**elevant (related to your ultimate vision), **T**ime (when you plan to reach your goal). These can be:
   **Educational Goals (school, certifications, etc.)**
   **Skill Goals (skills)**
   **Personal Goals (eliminating weaknesses)**
   **Promotional Goals**
   **Other Personal Goals (spouse, house, location)**
   **Financial Goals**

8. **Strategies** - Strategies are the individual *action steps* you'll take toAchieve your goals. These too should be specific and measurable.
   **Strategies to achieve educational goals**
   **Strategies to achieve skills goals**
   **Strategies to eliminate weaknesses**
   **Strategies to achieve your promotional goals**
   **Strategies to achieve other personal goals**
   **Strategies to achieve your financial goals**

9. **Implementation Plan** is a detailed listing of activities (steps), with the times the steps are to be completed and the cost to complete the step which will ultimately help you achieve your goals. If more than one person has a responsibility to help you achieve a step then the responsible person's name is listed by the action step. See sample format for implementation plan.

# Implementation Plan

| Goals | Action Steps | Start Date | Completion Date | Cost |
|-------|-------------|------------|-----------------|------|
| Obtain B.S Degree in Management | Take MG 320 | August 15 | December 15 | $2,500 |
| | Take MG 302 | | | |
| | Take MG 346 | | | |
| | Take MG 350 | | | |
| Obtain Project Management Cert | | | | |
| Overcome shyness | Read Ms. Kerner's Book - Do all exercises in Book | August 15 | December 15 | |
| | Start speaking to people who are standing or sitting by themselves | Immediately | | |
| | Read How to Win Friends and Influence People by Carnegie | Dec. 7 | Jan. 7, 16 | |

Laura Lynn Kerner has had a distinguished career with Internet software development companies and Healthcare organizations. Ms. Kerner was founder and CEO of an emergency management software development company. She served as Vice President and Consultant to software development companies in Atlanta and as an Executive and Consultant to hospitals and physician practices. She has been President of both professional and civic organizations and has been awarded many professional honors. She was elected President and later honored as a Distinguished Member of the Mississippi Health Information Management Association.

Ms Kerner now teaches marketing and international business at Athens State University, Athens, AL. She was awarded the highest award given for teaching, the Teaching Excellence Award and the Presidential Award for meritorious performance for sustained quality and excellence in performance of duties. She also received the Woman of Distinction Award from the North/Central Alabama Girl Scouts Association. Ms. Kerner has created a SUCCESS Program for "at-risk" kids and authored a book, My SUCCESS manual which is used by mentors in the program.

From personal experience in difficult and destructive relationships, Ms. Kerner came to learn that the most important key to being successful in business, in relationships and in life is the development of self-esteem. She has a unique way of using marketing principles, life experiences and humor to teach self-esteem development and life management skills.

Ms. Kerner is available for speaking engagements and for implementation of the SUCCESS program in middle, high schools, and colleges. She may be contacted via e-mail at lauralkerner@aol.com or via cell phone at 404-434-0062. **Website: www.laurakerner.com**